Native American Crafts

of the Northwest Coast, the Arctic, and the Subarctic

By Judith Hoffman Corwin

Franklin Watts
A Division of Scholastic Inc.

New York Toronto London Auckland Sydney
Mexico City New Delhi Hong Kong
Danbury, Connecticut

For Jules Arthur and Oliver Jamie . . .
and for the Native Americans
who have given us all these beautiful things—
drawings, paintings, sculptures, and songs of the Earth.

Book design by A. Natacha Pimentel C.

Library of Congress Cataloging-in-Publication Data
Corwin, Judith Hoffman.
    Native American crafts of the Northwest coast, the Arctic,
  and the Subarctic / by Judith Hoffman Corwin.
      p. cm.
     Includes index.
     Summary: Provides step-by-step instructions for craft
  projects based on traditional crafts of the Tlingit, Haida,
  Inuit, and other Native Americans of the Northwest Coast,
  Arctic, and Subarctic.
     ISBN 0-531-12201-8 (lib. bdg.)   0-531-15594-3 (pbk.)
     1. Indian craft—Juvenile literature. 2. Indians of North America—
Industries—Northwest, Pacific—Juvenile literature. 3 Indians of North
America—Industries—Alaska—Juvenile literature. 4. Indians of North
America—Industries—Canada, Northern—Juvenile literature. [1. Indian
craft. 2. Eskimo craft. 3. Handicraft.] I. Title.
TT22.c67 1999
745.5'08997—dc21   98-31471
                                                             CIP
                                                             AC

Contents

About the Native American Crafts Books

I arise from rest with movements swift
*   as the bear,*
*   as the raven's wings.*
I arise to meet the day.
My face is turned from the dark of night
*   to gaze at the dawn of the day*
*   now whitening in the sky.*

—Adapted from an Inuit song

Native Americans are believed to have been the first people to arrive on the North American continent thousands of years ago. They developed rich cultures based on their respect for the natural world around them—the Earth, sky, wind, rain, animals, plants, fire and water, the sun, the moon, and the stars.

The spirit of nature is important to Native Americans, and the design and decoration of the objects they use in their daily lives—to raise families, to farm, to hunt, to defend themselves, or to make war—reflect the elements of nature. The designs

on their clothing, pottery, baskets, dwellings, and weapons are decorative and are also an appeal to the goodwill of the spirits of the natural world. Native American people have no word for art because creating art is an integral part of life.

Now many Native Americans live in cities. Yet they often return to their home reservations to visit families and for special occasions. Their past is kept alive through storytelling and through arts and crafts. Traditional crafts, like the stories, are handed down from generation to generation, carrying along a cultural message.

The Native American Crafts series of books introduces young people to the cultures of Native Americans and to their creative work. We can learn about and appreciate Native American culture and incorporate what we learn into our lives through making art objects inspired by their examples. The projects in these books are based on crafts of everyday life, but do not involve ritual or religious objects. ◈

Native Americans of the Northwest Coast, the Arctic, and the Subarctic

The Northwest Coast

The Northwest Coast of the United States is a region rich in Native American myth and folklore. The area is a narrow strip of land along the Pacific Ocean, from Yakutat Bay in Alaska to the state of Washington. The Alaska current sweeps along the coast, producing a damp and fairly mild climate. The rugged country is covered with forests of cedars and firs. Steep mountain ranges border the inland area.

The coastal Native Americans were a settled people and harvested, preserved, and stored large amounts of salmon, their main food. Years ago, totem poles carved from giant cedar trees were powerful guardians of life in villages of the region. Today the totems inspire us with the power of the spirit world that they represent and the skill of those who carved them.

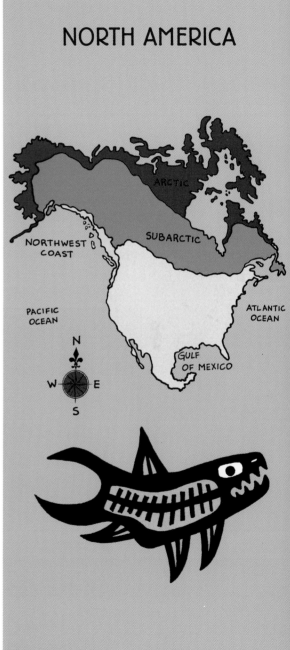

NORTH AMERICA

Several cultural groups live along the Northwest Coast. They are the Haida, the Tlingit, the Bella Coola, the Kwakiutl, the Tsimshian, the Coast Salish, and the West Coast People (or Nootka). They share cultural backgrounds, and live in similar environments.

The Arctic

Many of the people of the North American Arctic are called Inuit. The Inuit group includes two sub-groups: the Yup'ik and Inuit-Inupiaq.

Life is hard in the barren, icy lands of this region. Hunters follow the movements of the caribou, seal, walrus, and polar bear. The winters are long and dark and for several months of the year the sun does not shine. Inuit people live all through the Arctic, Alaska, northern Canada, Greenland, and Siberia.

The Aleut people, who also live in this region, share a common ancestry with the Inuit. They live on the chain of islands forming part of the land bridge between Alaska and Siberia. Human beings are believed to have crossed this bridge to reach the Western Hemisphere thousands of years ago.

The Subarctic

The Subarctic region of North America is south of the Arctic and includes Alaska and most of the interior of Canada. There are woodlands and swamps, mountains, lakes, and rivers. The long winters are bitterly cold, with short days, heavy snowfalls, and fierce winds. Summers are short, warm, and humid. Even though this region is harsh, it is home to Native Americans who have hunted and fished there for thousands of years. Their resourcefulness has helped them to survive and to create a special culture with beautiful arts and crafts. Native American groups of the Subarctic region include the Cree, Ingalik, and Ojibwa.

9

Northwest Coast Designs and Symbols

The Native Americans of the Northwest Coast show their special view of the world through their designs and art. Their region is rich, with plenty of fish and game. Because of the abundant food, an organized, settled society developed over time. Family rights and family ties are important. Each family has its own family crest made up of special animal designs.

Some people work as artists, making objects for the tribe. They create woven spruce-root hats, baskets, headdresses, ceremonial masks and bowls, blankets, carved boxes, and special storage trunks. The artists often work with cedar wood, which they carve and paint. Other materials—ivory, antlers, animal bones, stone, and metal—are worked in similar ways. The artists create abstract and bold designs. Each design image is made up of different parts that together tell a story. These traditional designs are either painted (two-dimensional) or sculpted (three-dimensional).

Animals are drawn with outlines. Their internal organs—hearts, stomachs, and other parts—are added in an "x-ray" style. Sometimes body parts are split up and arranged in an original way. Open spaces are decorated and filled with animal parts and other designs, such as faces. A series of S forms and U forms are used to connect design parts, to fill spaces, and to create details inside the outline of a creature.

Three colors are generally used. The outlines and the most important parts are drawn in black. Black defines the parts of the design—the head, eyes, eyebrows, nose, ears, tongue, wings, joints, tail, feathers, hands, claws, and feet. Red is used for elements that are next in importance. White is used as a background color. In modern works two more colors—blue-green and yellow—are sometimes used.

To see how the designs are made, look at the drawings here and then see how they are combined to make up beaver, whale, and human figures (pages 12-13). Other drawings (page 13) show nature patterns. We will use these designs in many of this book's projects. You can also experiment

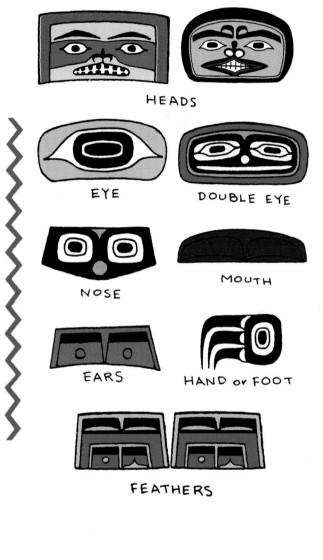

HEADS

EYE

DOUBLE EYE

NOSE

MOUTH

EARS

HAND or FOOT

FEATHERS

Here's What You Need:
- paper, poster paints, brushes, colored pencils, or markers
- T-shirt, cotton cloth
- homemade clay (page 47), or other materials as needed.

with them and draw them on T-shirts, greeting cards, bookmarks, book covers, and stationery. They can be used on clay tablets or clay bowls. Fill a large cotton cloth with a variety of designs to make a mural or wall hanging. ◈

BEAVER

PATTERNS FROM NATURE

BEAR TRACKS

FLYING GEESE

GOOSE TRACK

MOUNTAINS AND LAKES

WAVE

SANDHILLS

BERRIES

ARROWS

BACKBONE

CROSSINGS

TADPOLE

FISHING NET

BUTTERFLY

WHALE

HUMAN

13

Here's What You Need:
- wooden or cardboard box, pencil
- poster paints and brushes or colored permanent markers

Here's How You Do It:
- Find a solid color box or paint a box a solid color.
- Choose your designs and outline them in pencil on the box.
- Go over the lines with paint or colored markers. Color in parts of the design.

Treasure Box

The people of the Northwest Coast, Arctic, and Subarctic make containers to store materials they use—wood, bark, reeds, animal skins, and ivory from walrus tusks. The containers have decorative designs carved, painted, or drawn on them. Special containers are given away at traditional ceremonies on the Northwest Coast. The Inuit also give away boxes as presents. We will use traditional designs to decorate a box to hold special papers, souvenirs, or other treasures. Raven and grizzly bear designs are shown, or you can use designs from pages 10–13. ◆

RAVEN

GRIZZLY BEAR

Here's What You Need:
- heavy paper, pencil
- colored markers or crayons
- cardboard tubes (the largest you can find)
- scissors, glue, poster paint, brushes

Here's How You Do It:
- To make a paper totem pole, choose your designs and trace them (see page 46) or draw them freehand on paper, one above another. Go over the lines with markers or crayons. If you like, color in the designs. Roll the paper into a cylinder and glue the ends closed.
- To make a cardboard pole, find a large tube (commercial ice cream containers, poster or mailing tubes, are some possibilities) and paint it a solid color. Cut out your designs and glue them onto the tube, You can make miniature poles from paper-towel tubes or oatmeal boxes. You can also glue the designs onto small boxes.

16

Northwest Coast Totem Poles

Along the Northwest Coast, handsome totem poles mark the boundaries of Native American villages. Each has many designs, one carved above the other on a long pole—usually the trunk of a cedar tree. The designs may have mythical meanings, or may include a family crest and tell the family history of the pole's owner. The images are often stylized creatures—an eagle, hawk, bear, beaver, wolf—or a moon design. You need to look hard to separate the individual figures in the designs.

Tall totem poles also decorate the people's long, low, wooden houses. Three poles are usually placed in front of a house—one in the center, with an opening at ground level to serve as a front door, and two at the ends of the house. ◈

EAGLE

BEAR

HAWK

WOLF

BEAVER

17

Tlingit and Haida Baskets for a Potlatch

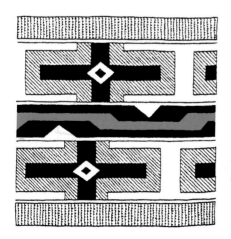

The potlatch is an important ceremony among Native Americans of the Northwest Coast. The potlatch is usually given by a chief or by a person with a high position in the tribe, to honor the traditions of the tribe. Some chiefs give a potlatch to announce the birth of an heir. The ceremony lasts several days and there is much feasting. Everyone wears ceremonial dress and carries rattles, masks, and drums. Inside a large hall, guests join in a dance enacting events from myths. Dancers portray bees, birds, bears, whales, and other creatures of the region.

Potlatch means "to give," and special objects, such as baskets, are created to be given away at the celebration. The Tlingit and Haida people of the Northwest Coast make baskets out of roots and strips of cedar bark. They decorate them with traditional designs using bands, diamonds, rectangles, triangles, and other forms. One design from a chief's basket hat shows a whale hunt. Other designs show a thunderbird and a lightning serpent. You can decorate a store-bought basket with Northwest Coast designs.

Here's What You Need:
- straw or wooden basket
- pencil
- permanent black and colored markers, or acrylic paint and brushes, newspaper

Here's How You Do It:
- Choose a design and sketch it with a pencil on the basket. Look at pages 10–13 for design ideas.
- Draw over your lines with a black marker or black acrylic paint. Acrylic paints can stain, so first spread newspapers over your working area.
- Paint in areas of your design to give it a personal touch.

Haida Creation Story Designs

A Haida legend tells of the creation of the Earth and of a great flood during which water covered the land. After the floodwaters went down, Raven went walking along the beach. Attracted by strange sounds, he discovered a giant clamshell with little beings wiggling inside. He crooned and coaxed them out, thus bringing the first human beings into the world. This story of the creation of humankind forms the design shown here. You can use it on note cards or enlarge it and paint it on a T-shirt.

Here's What You Need:
- pencil, paper, tracing paper
- T-shirt, cardboard
- colored fabric markers (for the T-shirt); colored markers or pencils (for note cards)

Here's How You Do It:
- To decorate a T-shirt, slide cardboard between the front and back of the shirt so the markers will not stain the back. Trace and transfer the design (page 46) to the shirt or copy it freehand. Use fabric markers to go over the lines. Color in areas of the design.
- For note cards, use a pencil to copy the design freehand onto a piece of paper, or trace it and transfer it to the paper (see page 46). Go over the lines with a black marker. Use colored markers to fill in the design.

21

Here's What You Need:
- empty coffee can or oatmeal box
- poster paints, brushes
- chamois cloth (available in hardware stores), leather, suede, Ultrasuede, or white fabric
- pencil, tracing paper, scissors
- black and colored markers
- rubber bands, string

Here's How You Do It:
- Paint the oatmeal box or coffee can a solid color and let it dry.
- Take the material you are using for the top of your drum and draw a circle on it 2 inches (5 cm) larger than the top of the can or box.
- Trace the design and transfer it (page 46) to the material, placing it in the center of the circle. Go over the design with a black marker. Color it in.
- Cut out the circle. Place it over the open end of the can or box. Secure it with rubber bands. Wrap the string over the rubber bands several times and tie the ends.

Haida Drum

This Haida raven design is graphic and bold. Painted on the top of a drum, it proudly proclaims the bird's presence! ◆

Miniature Inuit Carvings

The Inuit culture is made up of many groups of people. One group is the Netsilik, who live in the Canadian Arctic. *Netsilik* means "people of the seal," and the seal is important to these people. It provides meat, and oil for heat and light. The skins are used for clothing and for summer tents. Winter is seal-hunting season. The animals are harpooned as they come to their breathing holes in the ice.

During the long winter evenings, the hunters carve small animals out of ivory, animal bone or antlers, or stone. These carvings are believed to protect hunters and bring them luck. They are kept in animal skins and passed around when guests come or when stories are told. The figures are meant to be handled and their spirits shared. The designs here show a fish, seal, walrus, loon, fox, penguin, and polar bear.

Here's What You Need:
- pencil, tracing paper
- bar of white soap, tape, table or butter knife

Here's How You Do It:
- Trace one of the animal designs (page 46).
- Tape the drawing onto a large bar of white soap.
- Draw over the design with a pencil and remove the tracing paper. Make sure all of the design shows on the soap.
- With an adult helping, use the knife to carve away large sections of the soap until you have the rough shape of the animal. Now carefully carve around the animal design until you are satisfied. Etch in fish scales and other details with the knife. Carve out eyes and give your animals a smile.

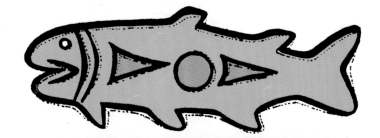

Sealskin Bracelet

The Central Canadian, Arctic Caribou, and Inuit people depend on caribou herds for food. In the fall—when the animals travel through their land—ceremonies are held to praise the caribou. In winter, the hunters build snow houses, or igloos. In warmer seasons they live in caribou-skin tents. We will use caribou or seal designs on a "sealskin" bracelet.

Here's What You Need:
- tan fabric, felt, Ultrasuede, suede, or chamois cloth (sold in hardware stores)
- pencil, tracing paper, black permanent marker
- hole punch
- string, yarn, or shoelace

Here's How You Do It:
- You need a piece of material 2 inches (5 cm) wide and long enough to go around your wrist plus 2 additional inches (5 cm).
- Choose a design. Trace it and transfer it onto the fabric (page 46), or draw it freehand. Draw over the lines with the black marker.
- With a hole punch, make a hole at each end of the fabric. Take a length of string or yarn or a shoelace about 7 inches (18 cm) long and run it through both holes. Tie the ends in a bow to close the bracelet.

25

Here's What You Need:
- cardboard or balsa wood (available at hobby or craft stores), 1/8 inch (3 mm) thick, 12 inches (30 cm) long, 3 inches (7.5 cm) wide
- tracing paper, pencil, black and colored markers

Here's How You Do It:
- With a pencil, copy the design or trace it and transfer it (page 46) onto the balsa wood or cardboard.
- Draw over the pencil lines with a black marker. Color in the design. A cardboard stick could be used as a bookmark.

Inuit Record Stick

Inuit people use ivory rods or sticks to keep records of important events. We will make a record stick that shows, in pictures, how people travel over the ice and snow and hunt animals. The Inuit use dog sleds pulled by teams of several husky dogs—up to twenty dogs for the largest sleds. Today, they use snowmobiles as well as sleds.

Life for the Inuit is very difficult in a world of endless snow, ice, and bitter cold. They use the few materials available to them with great skill and care. Until recently, paper was unavailable and the only wood they had was driftwood they found floating in the water. The Inuit believed this wood came from trees that grew at the bottom of the ocean.

Yup'ik Spirit Mask

The Yup'ik people of the western Subarctic believe that a spirit called Tunghak controls all the animals. A special mask (page 28) is worn during a ceremony to please Tunghak, and to ask for success in hunting and fishing. Traditionally the mask is made of wood, and has large eyes and a wide grin. Feathers surround the face and hands are attached to each side. Holes in the palms symbolize the releasing of the animals to the hunter. Animal figures are usually attached to the mask. ◈

(page 28)

Here's What You Need:
• paper plate, pencil, black marker, scissors, oaktag
• hole punch or nail
• yarn or string, feathers
• tracing paper, glue
• colored pencils or markers

Here's How You Do It:
• With a pencil, draw eyes and mouth on the paper plate. Go over the lines with a black marker. Cut holes in the center of the mouth and eyes.
• Outline your hands on oaktag. Cut out the hands. Draw circles in the palms and cut them out. Punch holes at the wrists and at the sides of the mask. Tie on the hands with strings.
• Trace and transfer the whale and bird designs to oaktag (page 46), or draw them freehand. Color them in and cut them out. Glue them to the mask.
• Make a hole at each side of the mask. Pull a string through each hole and knot the end. Use the strings to tie on the mask. Glue feathers around the face.

(page 46)

Inuit Stone Paintings

The Inuit people have a long tradition of painting and carving on a type of stone called soapstone. After outlining an animal shape, different patterns are used to decorate it. The simple circle-and-dot pattern shown here has been used since ancient times. We will draw traditional designs on stones that we can use as paperweights or decorative objects. ◆

Here's What You Need:
- smooth stones
- colored permanent markers

Here's How You Do It:
- Collect several smooth stones and wash and dry them.
- Using bright colored markers, draw animal designs on the stones. Choose from the animals the Inuit hunt—whale, skunk, owl, moose, reindeer, rabbit, and wolf. Other designs show a sun, patterns, trees, and a frog, lizard, and turtle.

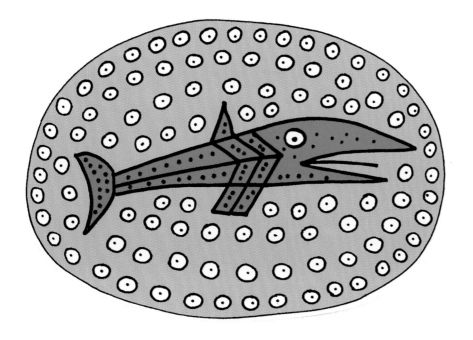

Here's What You Need:
- cardboard or clay (page 47)
- pencil, scissors, glue
- fine-line permanent markers
- 18 by 18 inch (45 by 45 cm) piece of leather, suede, Ultrasuede, felt, fabric, or chamois cloth
- string, bits of fur, shells, buttons, or stone,

Here's How You Do It:
- To make cardboard figures, outline the bodies and faces on cardboard. Cut them out. With fine-line markers, draw on the features of the faces.
- Use homemade clay (page 47) for clay figures. Pull off a handful of clay and shape each figure. Bake the figures and let them cool. With fine-line markers, draw in the faces.

Arctic and Subarctic Figures

The people of the Arctic and Subarctic regions use seal or reindeer skins to make loose outer garments for protection from the cold. They make waterproof pants, hooded parkas, boots, and mittens. The fur side of the skins is worn next to the body for added warmth.

The people of these regions invented the parka. This long, hooded jacket fits closely, with fur framing the face. Sometimes a narrow tail hangs down to the knees and a wide belt is tied around the waist. Underneath the parka, people wear tight, knee-length pants. Animal-skin stockings and boots, and tight-fitting outer boots, called mukluks, protect the feet. On a woman's parka, the hood is shaped like a pocket cradle to carry an infant. Of course everyone wears mittens to keep their hands warm.

Doll making is an important Inuit art form shared by men and women. We will make our dolls, or small figures, out of cardboard or clay, and dress them in parkas, pants, and mittens. ◆

- To dress your figures, draw the outlines of the clothes on a folded piece of material. Cut them out. You will have two pieces (a front and a back) for each garment.
- Glue the clothing onto the figures. Glue on stones, shells, string, bits of fur, and buttons to decorate the garments. The fun of this project is in creating little art pieces.

Here's What You Need:
- tracing paper, pencil
- large piece of solid-color felt or heavyweight fabric, or T-shirt
- black and colored fabric markers
- buttons, glue

Here's How You Do It:
- Trace the designs of the wave border and the whale and transfer them to the fabric or T-shirt (see page 46). If you like, draw them on freehand.
- Go over the lines with the black fabric marker.
- With a blue marker, color in the waves. Use yellow, blue, red, and green markers to color in the whale.
- Glue on the buttons.

Northwest Coast Whale Blanket

At special celebrations, such as the potlatch, button blankets are worn as shawls. The blankets are solid-color woolen blankets decorated with an appliquéd design, often of a creature of the Northwest Coast such as this whale. You can make a button blanket or shawl, or use the design on a T-shirt, too.

Here's What You Need:
- homemade clay (page 47)
- pencil
- acrylic paints and brushes, newspaper
- black fine-line permanent marker
- shoebox
- aluminum foil, silver glitter, scissors, glue

Here's How You Do It:
- Make a small dome shape out of a lump of clay. Poke a hole in the top for smoke to escape. Make a tunnel-shaped entrance. With a pencil, draw lines on the clay to show the "snow blocks."
- Paint the inside of a shoebox white. When it is dry, place the igloo in one corner of the box.

An Igloo Snow Scene

The Ingalik people are part of the Inuit cultural group that lives north of Hudson Bay in the Canadian Northwest. The name comes from their use of snow houses, or igloos. Today, they usually live in modern homes.

The Ingalik hunt whale, seal, walrus, and caribou. While hunting, they travel over large areas of the Arctic, living in temporary igloo villages and moving every few weeks. They can build a snow igloo in just hours. They cut blocks of ice from the ground and layer them in a spiral to form walls and a domed roof. A small tunnel is made for an entrance. Snow is melted and then frozen to create a clear block of ice for a window. Sled dogs are brought inside to help provide warmth in the winter. Our igloo scene will be made of clay.

- On aluminum foil, mix blue paint into white to make light blue. Use this to paint a sky and a circle shape for a hole in the ice. In winter, the Inuit fish through holes in the ice. With yellow, paint a sun.
- The Arctic ice and snow create a strong glare. Cut out shapes from aluminum foil and glue them into your scene. Spread a little glue on the ice and sprinkle on glitter.
- Make a clay seal and paint it brown. The Arctic and Subarctic figures (page 32) could also be placed in the foreground.

Here's What You Need:
- homemade clay (page 47)
- glue
- pencil, cardboard, scissors
- twig or toothpick, string
- acrylic paint, paintbrushes, newspaper
- clear nail polish

Here's How You Do It:
- Pinch off a handful of clay for a kayak. Shape the clay to points at the front and at the back. The bottom of the kayak is curved; the top is straight. Shape a hunter from another piece of clay.
- Bake the kayak and the hunter (page 47). When they are cool, glue the hunter into the boat.

Inuit Kayak

The Inuit invented the kayak—a type of covered canoe. It is small and easy to move, so a hunter can follow an animal through the water. One person sits in the center of the kayak, where there is a round opening in the cover. Around the opening, animal skins are tightly secured to keep out the water. We will make a miniature kayak and Inuit hunter out of clay.

- Draw a paddle and a fish on cardboard and cut them out. Use a pointed twig or a toothpick for the hunter's spear. With a pencil, make a small hole at the fish's mouth, and tie the string through it. Attach the other end of the string to the spear.
- Cover your working surfaces with newspaper. Paint and decorate the kayak and hunter. When dry, finish with a coat of clear nail polish.

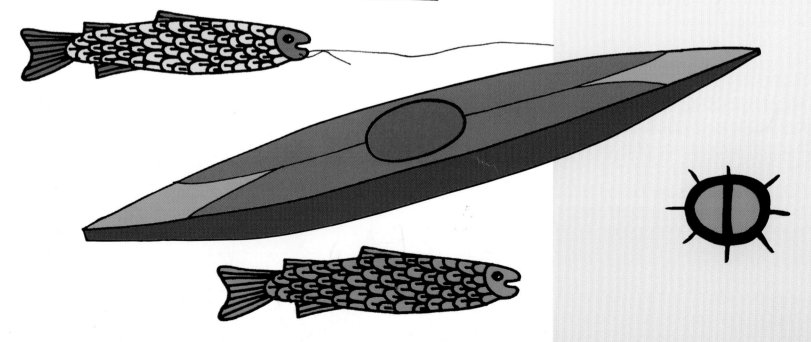

Here's What You Need:
- pencil, chopstick or stick
- paper cup, string
- black permanent marker (Sharpies work well on paper cups.)

Here's How You Do It:
- With a pencil, punch a hole near the rim of the paper cup. Tie a 20 inch long (50 cm) piece of string around one end of the pencil or a chopstick or stick. Thread the other end of the string through the hole in the cup and knot it.
- With a black marker, draw Inuit designs on the cup.
- To play the game, hold the stick in one hand, letting the cup fall loosely. Swing your hand and try to catch the cup on the stick. It takes practice. You can compete against a friend to see who can catch the cup on the stick more times in 2 or 3 minutes.

Canadian Inuit Game

In winter, the Inuit people play a game called *alaqaq*. The game is supposed to hasten the return of the sun after the long winter. It is also a good way to develop the hand-eye coordination needed for spear fishing. Traditionally, game pieces were made from the bones of the animals the Inuit hunted. Our game pieces are a paper cup and a pencil, chopstick, or stick.

Aleut Ices

Lone wolf
  On a snowy hillside
Icy, icy, snow drop,
  Drop,
    Drop,
    Drop.

—Aleut poem

In the far north, freshly fallen snow is scooped up and made into a kind of icy ice cream—crystal clear and cold. If you are lucky enough to live in the country and there is fresh snow, you can use it; otherwise crushed ice is wonderful. ◈

Here's What You Need:
- 4 cups fresh snow or ice cubes
- 1/2 cup confectioner's sugar
- 1 cup fresh or frozen strawberries
- measuring cups, spoons
- mixing bowl, spoon
- paper cupcake-tin liners

Here's How You Do It:
- Put the strawberries in a mixing bowl and mash them with a spoon.
- Collect some fresh snow or ask an adult to help you crush some ice cubes.
- Combine the confectioner's sugar, crushed ice or snow, and strawberries.
- Divide evenly into paper cupcake-tin liners, and enjoy!

41

Here's What You Need:
- pencil or black fine-line marker, paper
- colored pencils or markers

Here's How You Do It:
- Write one of these poems on a sheet of paper. Make a decorative border using some of the designs from this book. Experiment with different color pencils and markers. These decorated poems can be used on greeting cards or to make a poster or wall hanging.

Native American Writings

Tall Cedar Tree!
Clap your hands
*   and sing to me!*
Thank you, thank you.

Tall Cedar Tree!
Reach out your arms
*   and shelter me,*
Thank you, thank you.

—Northwest Coast

When Spring came,
With its wind gently blowing,
Leaves grew with a green fresh feeling,
And the warmth of the sun
Was beginning to be felt,
And the Animals of the Earth
Awoke, breathing the fresh new smell
Of life all over again.

—Tlingit

Look at me, friend!
I have come to ask
   for your dress,
   for you have come
   to take pity on us;
   for there is nothing
   for which you cannot be used,
   because it is your way
   that there is nothing
   for which we cannot use you,
   for you are really willing
   to give us your dress.
I have come to beg you,
   for this, long life-maker,
   for I am going to make
   a basket for lily roots out of you.

—Kwakiutl poem for gathering roots from a cedar tree

Sing your song
    looking up at the sky.
When I was young,
    every day was a beginning
    of some new thing,
    and every evening ended
    with the glow of the next day's dawn.
                                    —Subarctic

There is joy in
    feeling the warmth.
Come to the great world
    and seeing the sun
    follow its old footprints
    in the summer night.

There is fear
    feeling the cold.
Come to the great world.
Come to the great world
    and seeing the moon
    —now new moon, now full moon—
    follow its old footprints.
                                    —Arctic

44

You, whose day it is, make it beautiful.
Get out your rainbow colors.
So it will be beautiful.

—Nootka song to bring good weather

When I am grown, then I shall be a hunter,
O father!
Ya ha ha ha
When I am grown, I shall be a harpooner,
O father!
Ya ha ha ha
When I am grown, I shall be a canoe builder.
When I am grown, I shall be a carpenter.
When I am grown, I shall be an artisan.
That we may not be in want.

—Northwest Coast

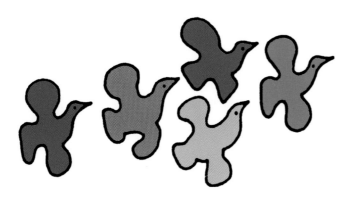

45

Basic Techniques

Tracing Designs

Here's What You Need:
- tracing paper
- pencil, tape
- drawing paper, fabric, or other material

Here's How You Do It:
- Place tracing paper over the design you want to trace. If you like, tape the paper down. Trace the lines of the design, pressing firmly on your pencil.
Remove the tape and turn the paper over. On the back, draw over the lines of the design with the side of your pencil point.
- Turn the tracing paper right side up and place it on a sheet of drawing paper or the material for your project. You may tape this down. Draw over the lines. This will transfer the design onto the paper or the material. ◈

Making Clay

Here's What You Need:
- 2 cups flour plus extra flour to sprinkle on the work surface
- 1 cup salt
- 1 cup water
- large bowl, spoon, measuring cup
- cookie sheet, potholders, aluminum foil

Here's How You Do It:
- Use this recipe to make clay for projects in this book. Additional instructions are given with the specific projects.
- Mix the flour and salt in a bowl. Add the water a little at a time. Mix the clay well with your hands until it is smooth. The clay is ready to roll out and cut, or to shape according to the project directions.
- If you need to bake the clay, ask an adult to help you use the oven. Heat the oven to 325° F. (165° C.). Line a cookie sheet with aluminum foil and place the clay pieces on it, spacing them 1 inch (2.5 cm) apart. Bake until lightly browned, 15 to 20 minutes, but check often to see that the edges are not burning.
- Using potholders, remove the cookie sheet from the oven. Allow the clay to cool. Paint or decorate it following the project instructions. ◆

Index